Distributed Shared Memory Consistency Models
Specification and Verification of
DSM Consistency Models using CADP

Venkateswarlu Chennareddy

2024

To my family and friends

Contents

List of Figures

List of Tables

Chapter 1

Introduction

Today, hardware and software systems are widely used in applications where failure is unacceptable: electronic commerce, telephone switching networks, air traffic control systems, medical instruments, and other examples too numerous to list. We frequently read of incidents where some failure is caused by an error in a hardware or software system. Clearly, the need for reliable hardware and software systems is critical. The success of the internet and embedded systems in automobiles, airplanes and other safety critical systems, we are likely to become even more dependent on the proper functioning of computing devices in the future. Because of this rapid growth in technology, it will become even more importance to develop methods that increase our confidence in the correctness of such systems.

1.1 Formal methods for Verification

The principle validation methods for complex systems are simulation, testing, deductive verification, and model checking [1]. Simulation and testing both involve making experiments before deploying the system in the field. While simulation is performed on an abstraction or a model of the system, testing is performed on the actual product. In both cases, these methods typically inject signals at certain points in the system and observe the resulting signals at other points. For software, simulation and testing usually involve providing certain inputs and observing the corresponding outputs. These methods can be cost-efficient way to find many errors. However, checking all of the possible interactions and potential pitfalls using simulation and testing techniques is rarely possible.

Deductive verification normally refers to the use of axioms and proof rules to prove the correctness of systems. In early research on deductive verification, the main focus was on guaranteeing the correctness of critical systems. The importance of deductive verification is widely recognized by computer scientists. It has significantly influenced the area of software development. For example, the notion of an invariant originated in research on deductive verification. However, deductive verification is a time consuming process that can be performed only by experts who are educated in logical reasoning and have considerable experience. Consequently, use of deductive verification is rare. An advantage of deductive verification is that it can be used for reasoning about infinite state systems.

Model checking is a technique for verifying finite state concurrent systems. One benefit of this restriction is that verification can be performed automatically. The procedure normally uses an exhaustive search of the state space of the system to determine if some specification is true or not. The procedure will always terminate with yes/no answer. Model checking consists of modeling, specification and verification steps. Although the restriction to finite state systems may seem to be a major disadvantage, model checking is applicable to several important classes of systems. An exciting new research direction [2] attempt to integrate deductive verification and model checking, so that the finite states of complex systems can be verified automatically.

1.2   Distributed Shared Memory

As the need for more computing power demanded by new applications constantly increases, systems with multiple processors are becoming a necessity. The gap between processor and memory speed is apparently widening, and that is why the memory system organization became one of the most critical design decisions to be made by computer architects. According to the memory system organization, systems with multiple processors can be classified into two large groups: shared memory systems and distributed memory systems.

In a shared memory system [3] (often called a tightly coupled multiprocessor), a single global physical memory is equally accessible to all processors. The ease of programming due to the simple and general programming model is the main advantage of this kind of systems. However, they typically suffer from increased contention in accessing the shared memory, especially in single bus topology, which limits their scalability. In addition to that, the design of the memory system tends to be more complex.

A distributed memory system (often called a multicomputer) consists of a collection of autonomous processing nodes, having an independent flow of control and local memory modules. Communication between processes

2

residing on different nodes is achieved through a message passing model, via a general interconnection network. Such a programming model imposes significant burden on the programmer, and induces considerable software overhead. On the other hand, these systems are claimed to have better scalability and cost effectiveness.

A distributed shared memory (DSM) [4] tries to combine the best of these two approaches. A DSM system logically implements shared memory model on a physically distributed memory system. This approach hides the mechanism of communication between remote sites from the application writer, so the ease of programming and the portability typical for shared memory systems, as well as the scalability and costeffectiveness of distributed memory systems, can be achieved with less engineering effort.

1.3   General DSM system structure

A DSM system generally involves a set of nodes or clusters, connected by an interconnection network is shown in Figure 1.1. A cluster itself can be uniprocessor or a multiprocessor system, usually organized around a shared bus [5]. Private caches attached to processors are virtually inevitable for reducing memory latency. Each system cluster contains a physical local memory module, which maps partially or entirely to the DSM globally address space. Regardless of topology bus, ring, mesh or local area network a specific interconnection controller in each cluster connect it into the system.

Information about states and current locations of particular data blocks usually resides in a system table or directory. Directory storage and organization are among most important design decision, greatly effect system scalability. Directory organization varies from full map storage to different dynamic organizations, such as single or double linked lists and trees. No matter the organization, the cluster provides storage either for the entire directory or part of it. In this way, the system directory can distribute across the system as a flat or hierarchical structure. In hierarchical topologies, if cluster on intermediate level exist, they usually contain only directories and the corresponding interface controllers. Directory organization and the semantics of information kept in directories depend on the applied method for maintaining data consistency.

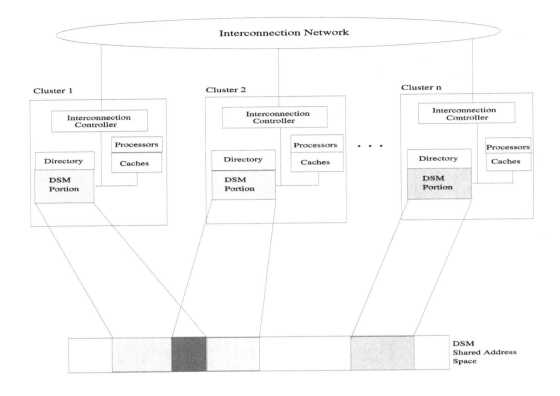

Figure 1.1: Structure and Organization of a DSM system

1.4   Key Issues in DSM System

There are three key issues when accessing data items in the DSM address space, while keeping the data consistent:

- DSM algorithm

- Implementation level of DSM mechanism

- What is the memory consistency model

The crucial objective of solving those problems is the minimization of the average access time to the shared data. Having this goal in mind, two strategies for distribution of shared data are most frequently applied: replication and migration. Replication allows that multiple copies of the same data item reside in different local memories, in order to increase the parallelism in accessing logically shared data. Migration implies a single copy of data item which has to be moved to the accessing site, counting on the locality of reference in parallel applications. Besides that, just as in shared-memory systems with private caches, systems with distributed shared memory have to deal with the consistency problem, when replicated copies of the same data exist. In order to preserve the coherent view of shared address space, according to the strict consistency semantics, a read operation must return the most recently written value. Therefore, when one of multiple copies of data is written, the others become stale, and have to be invalidated or updated, depending on the applied coherence policy. Although the strict coherence semantics provides the most natural view of shared address space, various weaker forms of memory consistency can be applied in order to reduce latency. Simultaneous existence of multiple copies of the same data, that some of the DSM algorithms allow, imposes additional problem of keeping those copies consistent.

1.5   Motivation

As the need for more computing power demanded by new applications constantly increases, systems with multiple processors are becoming a necessity. However, it seems that the programming of such systems still requires significant efforts and skills. The commercial success of multiprocessors and distributed systems will be highly dependent on favors of the programming paradigms they offer. In this direction, numerous ongoing research efforts are focused on an increasingly attractive class of parallel computer systems - distributed shared memory systems. Today, hardware and software systems are widely used in applications where failure is unacceptable. Clearly the need for reliable hardware and software systems is critical. Distributed shared memory working and its data consistency is very important. We have to explore the all possible errors and thorough testing of data consistency in DSM System is essential. Only possible way to do that is formal verification of DSM Consistency models. At present more research going on verification of consistency models in DSM System. Up to now, most reported successes have been either for far simpler memory models such as cache coherence or Sequential consistency [6]. So, In this work we are attempted to verify weak consistency model of DSM System.

1.6 Objective

The objective of this work is Specification and Verification of Distributed Shared Memory Weak Consistency. For this, we designed and implemented abstract Distributed Shared Memory (DSM) System. Formal Specification of Weak Consistency properties and these consistency properties are verified using Construction and Analysis of Distributed Processes (CADP) Tool box.

1.7 Organization

The remaining part of this work is organized as follows. In Chapter 2, we mentioned memory stency models and verification of consistency models. In Chapter 3, we have given LOTOS language description and CADP tool box overview. In Chapter 4, we proposed an approach for Verification of Relaxed Consistency Models for that we designed and implemented Abstract DSM System. We specified and verified weak consistency properties and results are shown. In Chapter 5, we have concluded our work and given future directions.

Chapter 2

Related Work

The memory consistency model [7] defines the legal ordering of memory references issued by a processor, as observed by other processor. Different types of parallel applications inherently require various consistency models. The models restrictiveness largely influences the system performance in executing these applications. Basically memory consistency models divided into two types: Strong and Relaxed consistency models. *Sequential* and *processor* consistency comes under Strong consistency models. *Weak, release, lazy release* and *entry* consistency comes under relaxed consistency models. Stronger forms of the consistency model typically increase memory access latency and bandwidth requirements, while simplifying programming. Looser constraints in more relaxed models, which allow memory reordering, pipelining, and overlapping, consequently improve performance, at the expense of higher programmer involvement in synchronizing shared data accesses. For optimal behavior, systems with multiple consistency models adaptively applied to appropriate data types have recently emerged. Stronger memory consistency models that treat synchronization accesses as ordinary read and write operations are *sequential* and *processor* consistency. More relaxed models that distinguish between ordinary and synchronization accesses are *weak, release, lazy release* and *entry* consistency.

2.1   Sequential Consistency

Lamport [8] defines *Sequential Consistency* (SC) as follows: A system is sequentially consistent if the result of any execution is the same as if the operations of all the processors were executed in some sequential order, and the operations of each individual processor appear in this sequence in the order specified by its program.

Sufficient Conditions for Sequential Consistency are

- Before a READ is allowed to perform with respect to any other processor, all previous READ accesses must be globally performed and all previous WRITE accesses must be performed, and

- Before a WRITE is allowed to perform with respect to any other processor, all previous READ accesses must be globally performed and all previous WRITE accesses must be performed.

2.2   Processor Consistency

To relax some of the orderings imposed by sequential consistency, Goodman introduces the concept of *Processor Consistency* (PC) [9]. Processor consistency requires that writes issued from a processor may not be observed in any order other than that in which they were issued. However, the order in which writes from two processors occur, as observed by themselves or a third processor, need not be identical. Processor consistency is weaker than sequential consistency; therefore, it may not yield correct execution if the programmer assumes sequential consistency. However, Goodman claims that most applications give the same results under the processor and sequential consistency models. Specifically, he relies on programmers to use explicit synchronization rather than depending on the memory system to guarantee strict event ordering.

Conditions for Processor Consistency are

- Before a READ is allowed to perform with respect to any other processor, all previous READ accesses must be performed, and

- Before a WRITE is allowed to perform with respect to any other processor, all previous accesses READs and WRITEs must be performed.

2.3   Weak Consistency

A Weaker Consistency model can be derived by relating memory request ordering to synchronization points in the program. As an example, consider a processor updating a data structure within a critical section. If the computation requires several WRITE accesses and the system is sequentially consistent, then each WRITE will have to be delayed until the previous WRITE is complete. But such delays are unnecessary because the programmer has already made sure that no other process can rely on that data structure being consistent until the critical section is exited. Given that all synchronization points are identified, we only need to ensure that the memory is consistent at those points. This scheme has the advantage of providing the user with a reasonable programming model, while permitting multiple memory accesses to be pipelined. The disadvantage is that all synchronization accesses must be identified by the programmer or compiler.

The *Weak Consistency* (WC) model proposed by Dubois et al. [10] is based on the above idea. They distinguish between ordinary shared accesses and synchronization accesses, where the latter are used to control concurrency between several processes and to maintain the integrity of ordinary shared data.

Conditions for Weak Consistency are

- Before an ordinary READ or WRITE access is allowed to perform with respect to any other processor, all previous *synchronization* accesses must be performed, and

- Before a *synchronization* access is allowed to perform with respect to any other processor, all previous ordinary READ and WRITE accesses must be performed, and

- *Synchronization* accesses are sequentially consistent with respect to one another.

2.4 Release Consistency

The *Release Consistency* (RC) Model proposed by Gharachorloo et al. [11] is an extension of weak consistency that exploits the information about acquire, release, and non-synchronization accesses. Four of the ordering restrictions in weak consistency are not present in release consistency. The first is that ordinary READ and WRITE accesses following a release access do not have to be delayed for the release to complete. The purpose of the release synchronization access is to signal that previous accesses in a critical section are complete, and it does not have anything to say about ordering of accesses following it. Of course, the local dependences within the same processor must still be respected. Second, an acquire synchronization access need not be delayed for previous ordinary READ and WRITE accesses to be performed. Since an acquire access is not giving permission to any other process to read/write the previous pending locations, there is no reason for acquire to wait for them to complete. Third, a non-synchronization special access

9

does not wait for previous ordinary accesses and does not delay future ordinary accesses; a non-synchronization access does not interact with ordinary accesses. The fourth difference arises from the ordering of special accesses. In release consistency, they are only required to be processor consistent and not sequentially consistent. For all applications that we have encountered, sequential consistency and processor consistency (for special accesses) give the same results.

Conditions for Release Consistency are

- Before an ordinary READ or WRITE access is allowed to perform with respect to any other processor, all previous *acquire* accesses must be performed, and

- Before a *release* access is allowed to perform with respect to any other processor, all previous ordinary READ and WRITE accesses must be performed, and

- *Special accesses* are processor consistent with respect to one another.

2.5 Lazy Release Consistency

Lazy Release Consistency (LRC) is proposed by Keleher et al. [12] is based on Release Consistency. A relaxed memory consistency model that permits a processor to delay making its changes to shared data visible to other processors until subsequent synchronization accesses occur. Essentially all shared accesses are divided into ordinary accesses, acquire synchronization accesses, and release synchronization accesses. Release consistency allows the results of ordinary shared writes to be buffered locally until the next release operation.

LRC is a refinement of RC that allows consistency action to be postponed until a synchronization variable released in a subsequent operation is acquired by another processor. Synchronization transfers in an LRC system, therefore involve only the synchronizing processors. A release in an eager RC system requires the releasing processor to make its shared writes visible to all other processors in the system that caches the data. This reduction in synchronization traffic can result in a significant decrease in the total amount of system communication, and a consequent increase in overall performance.

Conditions for Lazy Release Consistency are

- Before an ordinary READ or WRITE access is allowed to perform with respect to another process all previous *acquire* accesses must be performed with respect to that other process, and

10

- Before a *release* access is allowed to perform with respect to any other process, all previous ordinary READ and WRITE accesses must be performed with respect to that other process, and

- *sync* are sequentially consistent with respect to one another.

2.6 Entry consistency

Another consistency model that has been designed to be used with critical sections is *Entry Consistency* (EC) is proposed by Bershad et al. [13]. It requires the programmer to use acquire and release at the start and end of each critical section, respectively. However, unlike release consistency, entry consistency requires each ordinary shared variable to be associated with some synchronization variable such as a lock or barrier. If it is desired that elements of an array be accessed independently in parallel, then different array elements must be associated with different locks. When acquire is done on a synchronization variable, only those ordinary shared variables guarded by that synchronization variable are made consistent. Entry consistency differs from lazy release consistency in that the latter does not associate shared variables with locks or barriers and at acquire time has to determine empirically which variables it needs.

Conditions for entry consistency are

- An *acquire* access of a synchronization variable is not allowed to perform with respect to a process until all updates to the guarded shared data have been performed with respect to that process.

- Before an exclusive mode access to a synchronization variable by a process is allowed to perform with respect to that process, no other process may hold the synchronization variable, not even in nonexclusive mode.

- After an exclusive mode access to a synchronization variable has been performed, any other process next nonexclusive mode access to that synchronization variable may not be performed until it has performed with respect to that variable's owner.

2.7 Performance Analysis of Memory Consistency Models

As per performance results given in [14], the SC model have lowest performance amongst all memory consistency models. The PC model requires to use larger write buffers, while the WC and RC models require smaller write buffers. The PC model may perform even lower than the SC model, if a small buffer was used. The performance of the WC model depends heavily on the synchronization rate in user code. For a low synchronization rate, the WC model performs as well as the RC model. With sufficient multithreading and network bandwidth, the RC model shows the best performance among the above four models. The performance of EC and LRC are better than above four models. If we consider performance of EC and LRC, performance advantages of one or the other highly depend on the application [15].

2.8 Verification of Consistency Models

We have mentioned closely related work, pertaining to finite state verification of protocols with respect to consistency. Graf [16] introduced a verification approach for sequential consistency. They gave a set of properties expressible as temporal logic formulas such that any system satisfying them is a sequential consistent memory. Then, they verified these properties on a distributed cache memory by means of verification method. We designed and implemented abstract DSM Sytem. Then, we verified weak consistency properties on abstract DSM. So, our approach is similar to Graf's approach. Rob Gerth [17] proposed a very similar approach to ours, using a lazy caching algorithm and sequential consistency.

Henzinger et al. [18] proposed an approach for verifying sequential consistency on shared-memory multiprocessor systems. To verify sequential consistency of memory systems with an arbitrary number of processors, locations and data values using a model checker. They have considered two specific memory protocols, namely the lazy caching protocol and a snoopy cache coherence protocol. Shaz Qadeer [19] proposed an approach for verifying sequential consistency on shared memory multiprocessor systems by model checking. They presented a model checking algorithm to verify sequential consistency on systems for a finite number of processors and memory locations and an arbitrary number of data values. Condon et al. [20] proposed a verification approach based on logical clocks to automatable verification of sequential consistency.

Recently, P. Chatterjee et al. [21] proposed an approach to specification and verification framework for developing weak shared memory consistency protocols. In this paper, the method was applied to four snoopy-bus protocols for implementing aspects of the Alpha and Itanium memory models. They verified snoopy-bus protocols specifically for Alpha and Itanium memory models. But, we verified weak consistency memory model for general abstract DSM Sytem. So, our approach is different from Chatterjee et al. approach. R.P. Ghughal et al. [22] proposed an approach to Verification Methods for Weaker Shared Memory Consistency Models. In this, they constructed an architectural testing programs similar to those constructed by Collier suited for weaker memory models. Their work was mainly focused on architectural tests for weaker memory models and the new abstraction methods to construct test automata for weaker memory models. P. Chatterjee et al. [6] proposed a formal approach to verify protocol implementation models against weak shared memory models through automatable refinement checking supported by a model checker. They verified four different alpha and Itanium memory model implementation against their respective specifications. They used it to check for the existence of a refinement mapping between an implementation model and an abstract model.

Chapter 3

CADP Overview

CADP [23] (*Construction and Analysis of Distributed Processes*) is a popular toolbox for the design of communication protocols and distributed systems. CADP is developed by the VASY team at INRIA, France.

CADP offers a wide set of functionalities, ranging from step by step simulation to massively parallel model-checking. It is the only toolbox to offer:

- Compilers for several input formalisms, e.g.:

  1. High level protocol descriptions written in the ISO language LOTOS [International Standard 8807]. The toolbox contains two compilers (CAESAR and CAESAR.ADT) that translate LOTOS descriptions into C code to be used for simulation, verification, and testing purposes.

  2. Low level protocol descriptions specified as finite state machines.

  3. Networks of communicating automata, i.e., finite state machines running in parallel and synchronized together (either using process algebra operators or synchronization vectors).

- Several equivalence checking tools (minimization and comparisons modulo bisimulation relations), such as BCG_MIN and BISIMULATOR.

- Several verification algorithms combined together: enumerative verification, on-the-fly verification, symbolic verification using binary decision diagrams, compositional minimization, partial orders, distributed model checking, etc.

- Plus a bunch of other tools with advanced functionalities such as visual checking, performance evaluation, etc.

3.1 LOTOS (Language Of Temporal Order Specification)

LOTOS [24, 25] is a specification language that has been specifically developed for the formal description of the OSI (Open systems Interconnection) architecture, although it is applicable to distributed, concurrent systems in general. In LOTOS a system is seen as a set of processes which interact and exchange data with each other and with their environment.

3.1.1 Basic LOTOS

Basic LOTOS only describes process synchronization, while full LOTOS also describes inter process value communication. The program structure of LOTOS shown in Figure 3.1. An essential component of a process definition is

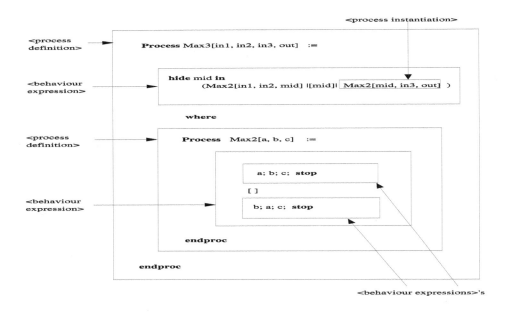

Figure 3.1: Definition of process Max3

its behaviour expression. A behaviour expression is built by applying an operator (e.g., []) to other behaviour expressions. A behaviour expression may also include instantiations of other processes (e.g. Max2), whose definitions are provided in the **where** clause following the expression. Given behaviour expression B, we will allow calling B also a process, for convenience, even when no process name is explicitly associated with the behaviour expressed by B.

The complete list of basic LOTOS behaviour expressions is given in Table 3.1, which includes all basic LOTOS operators. Symbols B, B1, B2 in the table stand for any behaviour expression. Any behaviour expression must match one of the formats listed in column SYNTAX. We have taken the metalinguistic liberty of representing some lists with dots. By inspecting Table 3.1 we may observe that basic LOTOS includes nullary operators (e.g. inaction), unary operators (e.g. action prefix), binary operators (e.g. parallel composition), and two behaviour expressions.

NAME	SYNTAX
Inaction	stop
Action prefix	
-Unobservable (internal)	i ; B
-Observable	g; B
Choice	B1[]B2
Parallel composition	
-General case	B1 [g1, ... , gn] B2
-Pure interleaving	B1 ||| B2
-Full synchronization	B1 || B2
hiding	hide g1, ... , gn in B
Process instantiation	p [g1, ... ,gn]
Successful termination	exit
Sequential composition (enabling)	B1 ≫ B2
Disabling	B1 [B2

Table 3.1: Syntax of behaviour expressions in basic LOTOS

3.1.2 Full LOTOS

The integration of *type definitions* and *process definitions* in a full LOTOS specification is illustrated in Program 3.1, which shows the syntax of a typical *specification* and a typical *process definition*.

Specification:

specification typicalSpec [gate list] (parameter list) : functionality
    type definitions
behaviour
    behaviour expression
where

16

> type definitions
> process definitions
> **endspec**

process definition:

> **process** typicalProc [gate list] (parameter list) : functionality :=
> *behaviour expression*
> **where**
> type definitions
> process definitions
> **endspec**

Program 3.1: LOTOS Program Structure

Process and *type definitions* may appear in the **where** clause of a *specification* or *process definition*, in either order or even interleaved. It clearly appears that a *specification* and a *process definition* have a similar structure. A minor difference is that the *behaviour expression* is preceded by the keyword **behaviour** in the first case, and by the definition symbol ':=' in the second case. A more significative difference is that some *type definitions* may appear before the *behaviour expression* of a *specification*, whereas this is not allowed in a *process definition*. Such *type definitions* are meant to be global definitions, which can be referenced in the *parameter list* of the *specification*.

3.2 CADP Tools Overview

The CADP toolbox contains several closely interconnected components:

3.2.1 CAESAR

CAESAR [26] is a compiler that translates the behavioral part of a LOTOS specification into either a C program (to be executed or simulated) or into an LTS (to be verified using bisimulation tools and/or temporal logic evaluators). For instance, one can check the LTS of a protocol against the LTS of the service implemented by the protocol. Both LTSs are generated using CAESAR and compared using ALDEBARAN. It is also possible to specify protocol properties using temporal logic formulas that can be evaluated on the protocol LTS. The current version of CAESAR allows the generation of large LTSs (some million states) within a reasonable lapse of time. Moreover, the efficient compiling algorithms of CAESAR can also be exploited in the framework of the OPEN/CAESAR environment. The most recent version of CAESAR provides a functionality called EXEC/CAESAR for C code generation. This C code interfaces with the real world, and can be embedded in applications. This allows rapid prototyping directly from the LOTOS specification.

3.2.2   CAESAR.ADT

CAESAR.ADT [27] is a compiler that translates the data part of LOTOS specifications into libraries of C types and functions. Each LOTOS sort is translated into an equivalent C type and each LOTOS operation is translated into an equivalent C function (or macrodefinition). CAESAR.ADT also generates C functions for comparing and printing abstract data types values, as well as iterates for the sorts the domain of which is finite. CAESAR.ADT is fast translation of large programs (several hundreds of lines) is usually achieved in a few seconds. CAESAR.ADT can be used in conjunction with CAESAR, but it can also be used separately to compile and execute efficiently large abstract data types descriptions.

3.2.3   ALDEBARAN

ALDEBARAN [28] is a tool for verifying communicating systems, represented by labelled transition systems (LTS), i.e., transition machines the transitions of which are labelled by action names. It allows the reduction of LTSs modulo various equivalence relations (such as strong bisimulation, observational equivalence, delay bisimulation, tau*.a bisimulation, branching bisimulation, and safety equivalence). It also allows to perform comparison according to strong bisimulation preorder, tau*.a preorder, or safety preorder.The verification algorithms used in ALDEBARAN are based either on the Paige-Tarjan algorithm for computing the relational coarsest partition, or on the on-the-fly techniques proposed by Fernandez-Mounier, or on symbolic LTS representation using Binary Decision Diagrams (BDDs), or on compositional algorithms. ALDEBARAN has diagnosis capabilities that provide the user with explanations when two LTSs are found to be not equivalent.

3.2.4   BCG

BCG [29] (Binary-Coded Graphs) is both a format for the representation of explicit LTSs and a collection of libraries and programs dealing with this format. Compared to ASCII based formats for LTSs, the BCG format uses a binary representation with compression techniques resulting in much smaller (up to 20 times) files. BCG is independent from any source language but keeps track of the objects (types, functions, variables) defined in the source programs.

3.2.5 XTL

XTL [30] (eXecutable Temporal Language) is a functional like programming language designed to allow an easy, compact implementation of various temporal logic operators. These operators are evaluated over an LTS encoded in the BCG format. Besides the usual predefined types (Booleans, integers, etc.), the XTL language defines special types, such as sets of states, transitions, and labels of the LTS. It offers primitives to access the information contained in states and labels, to obtain the initial state, and to compute the successors and predecessors of states and transitions. The temporal operators can be easily implemented using these functions together with recursive user-defined functions working with sets of states and/or transitions of the LTS. A prototype compiler for XTL has been developed, and several temporal logics like HML, CTL, ACTL and LTAC have been easily implemented in XTL.

3.2.6 EUCALYPTUS

EUCALYPTUS [31] is a graphical user interface written in Tcl/Tk that integrates CADP is shown in Figure 3.2. This interface has the name of the project within which it was developed: the euro-canadian project "EUCALYPTUS"

3.2.7 SVL

SVL [32] (Script Verification Language) is a scripting language that targets at simplifying and automating the verification of LOTOS programs. SVL behaves as a toolindependent coordination language on top of the CADP and FC2 tools, in the same way as EUCALYPTUS is a tool-independent graphical user interface. SVL offers high-level operators for generation, parallel composition, minimization, label hiding, label renaming, abstraction, comparison, and model-checking of LTSs. It supports several methods of verification (e.g., enumerative, compositional, and on-the-fly), which can be easily combined together. A compiler for SVL has been developed, which translates an SVL verification scenario into a Bourne shell script, which will perform all the operations needed to execute the verification scenario, e.g.,

3.2.9 TGV

A tool for the generation of conformance test suites based on verification technology TGV [34] takes as entries a description of a protocol's behaviour and a test purpose, which selects the subset of the protocol's behaviour to be tested. It produces test suites. which are used to assess the conformance of a protocol implementation with respect to the formal specification of the protocol.

Chapter 4

Verification of Weak Consistency

4.1 Design and Implementation of Abstract DSM System

The architecture of Abstract DSM System M_{dsm} is depicted in Figure 4.1. Abstract DSM M_{dsm} consists of a DSM address space and n processors, each processor associated with local DSM portion. Each local Memory M_i contains a part of DSM memory and has two queues associated with it: Out queue Out_i in which P_i's write request are buffered and In queue In_i in which pending local DSM updates are stored. The arrows indicate the information flow from Out queue to In queue and DSM.

The data structures include DSM Address Space and the following:
n pairs of unbounded FIFO queues, or lists, In_i and Out_i, the entries in which are either (data, address) or (data, address, *) where * stands for either 0 or 1. These queues have the following operations:

- *append(queue, item)* adds item as the last entry in queue.

- *first(queue)* returns the first entry in queue.

- *tail(queue)* returns the result of removing first(queue) from queue.

- { } denotes the empty queue.

- *queue[i]* denotes the ith element of queue where queue[0]=first(queue).

The initial states of M_{dsm} are those in which all queues are empty.

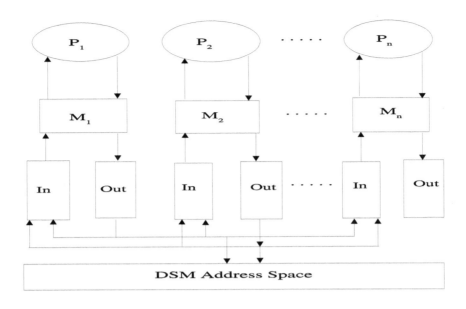

Figure 4.1: Architecture of Abstract DSM System M_{dsm}

In our program formalism, the Abstract DSM System M_{dsm} can be described as a set of processes of the form $P_1 \mathbin{|||} P_2 \mathbin{|||} P_3 \mathbin{|||} \cdots\cdots \mathbin{|||} P_n$ where each process P_i is defined as follows.

Process Name: P_i

Variables: Input: a: address, d: datum

Local: M_i: memory of address × datum (local memory)

Out_i: buffer of address × $datum_i$

Shared: In_i: buffer of address × datum, boolean i: index

DSM: memory of address × datum (Distributed Shared Memory)

Transitions:

$init$ $\forall a \in address \cdot empty(Out_i) \wedge empty(In_i) \wedge$
$holds(M_i,(a,null)) \wedge holds(DSM,(a,null))$

$write_i(a,\ d)$ $append(Out_i,\ (a,\ d),\ Out'_i)$

$read_i(a,\ d)$ $empty(Out_i) \wedge notBoolOne(In_i) \wedge holds(M_i,\ (a,\ d))$

$mw_i(a,\ d)$ $first(Out_i,(a,\ d)) \wedge tail(Out_i\ ,(a,\ d),\ Out'_i) \wedge$
$update(DSM,\ (a,\ d),\ DSM') \wedge$
$\forall k \in index \cdot append(In_i,\ ((a,\ d),\ i{=}k),\ In'_i)$

23

$mr_i(a, d)$ $\qquad$ $holds(M_i, (a, null)) \wedge holds(DSM, (a, d)) \wedge$
$\qquad\qquad\qquad$ $\neg isin(In_i, (a, d)) \wedge append(In_i,((a,d),0),In_i')$

$du_i(a, d)$ $\qquad$ $first(In_i,(a,d)) \wedge tail(In_i,(a,d),In_i') \wedge update(M_i,(a,d),M_i')$

$dl_i(a)$ $\qquad$ $clear(M_i,a,M_i')$

$sync$ $\qquad$ $empty(Out_i) \wedge empty(In_i)$

Explanation for the functions used above is given here:

$update(M_i,(a,d),M_i')$ is equivalent to $M_i'=update(M_i,(a,d))$, means update local memory M_i in address location a with datum d, we will call local memory after update M_i'.

$notBoolOne(In_i)$ function is used to determine is there any entry in In_i queue is of the form (*, *, 1). Then function notBoolOne(In_i) returns true value if In_i queue contains entry of the form (*, *, 1), otherwise it returns false.

$holds(M_i,(a,d))$ function used to determine at address location a contains datum d in local memory M_i, if available then it will return true otherwise it will return false value.

$isin(In_i,(a,d))$ function returns true value if entry (a,d,b) where b is boolean value is available some where in queue In_i.

$clear(M_i,a,M_i')$ set datum to null at address a in local memory M_i.

$empty(Out_i)$ function returns true value if Out queue of Process P_i is empty.

$empty(In_i)$ function returns true value if In queue of Process P_i is empty.

Process P_i wants to perform a write operation then add an entry (a, d) to Out_i queue. Process P_i wants to perform a read operation Out_i queue must be empty and In_i queue doesn't have an entry of this form (*, *, 1) and local memory M_i contains an entry (a, d) then read operation proceed further. For memory write operation of process P_i, removes an entry from Out_i queue and update its value in DSM global address space and then add an entry in all remaining processes In queues with an entry (a, d, 0) and add an entry (a, d, 1) to In queue of process P_i. Process P_i wants to perform a memory read operation, DSM global memory has an entry (a, d) and local memory M_i doesn't have value at address location a and process P_i's In queue doesn't have an entry (a, d) then add an entry (a, d, 0) to In queue of Process P_i. To perform Process P_i local memory update operation, removes an entry from In queue of Process P_i and update its local memory M_i. For local memory invalidate operation, we just clear an entry (a, d) in local memory M_i. For synchronization operation we have to complete all operations that are there in both In_i and Out_i queues. If we want to perform sync operation In_i and Out_i queues must be empty. LOTOS also provides built in synchronization operation to perform synchronization operation between processes. Just, we have mentioned where we want synchronization between the processes. For example we want synchronization between Process P_i and Process P_j at read operation, then we will mention this as P_i $||[\text{read}]||$ P_j.

4.2 Specification and Verification of Weak Consistency properties

To verify Weak Consistency properties of DSM System, we need to specify Weak Consistency properties in temporal logic. This is one way of verification of properties. Another way of verification of properties is to identify the states involved in the properties that we want to verify, and then hide the all states in abstract DSM LTS except those states required in that property. After that, apply strong reduction on abstract DSM System. Then, we described that property in states and transitions. Compare Observation Equivalence of these two systems, abstract DSM system and property written in sates and transitions. SVL provides these features i.e. comparison of Observational Equivalence and Strong Reduction. If these two systems are Observationally Equivalent then it terminate with TRUE result, otherwise property not satisfied some where in the system and terminate with FALSE result. Third way of verifying the properties is to write property in temporal logic either in XTL or mu-calculus form. Then, SVL provides facility to verify that property written in temporal logic directly in LOTOS program. We verified weak consistency properties in various ways.

In weak consistency, when ever Process P_i writes some value then Process P_j wants to read the same value then Process P_j has to get the latest value written by Process P_i. We will say this as in every process $write_i$(a, d) has occurred, then $read_j$(a, d) has to wait until (a, d) available, where index i indicate the process P_i performing the event, a is address of the memory

25

element and d is data element. Formal specification of this property specified here in terms of ∀CTL.

(P1)   ∀(a,d) ∈ address × data, ∀i ∈ index
        $init \Rightarrow \mathbf{AG}[after(write(a,d)) \Rightarrow (\neg enable(read(a,d))) \mathbf{U} avail(a,d)]$

We verified property P1 in three ways. In first method, Property P1 written in mu-calculus form. Caesar compiler convert LOTOS program of abstract DSM system into LTS System. We verified Property P1 in LTS. It will check in all possible cases in LTS. If this property satisfied in all cases then it will give TRUE result. If some where this property not satisfied then it will terminate with FASLE output. Property P1 written in mu-calculus form here.

(P1)   [true*. "write" . (not " du ")* . "read"] false

In second method of verification of Property P1 is, Caesar compiler translate abstract DSM system in LOTOS to LTS in BCG format. Then, hide the all states except *read, write* and *du* of DSM LTS. After that, applied strong reduction on LTS System. We described Property P1 in states and transitions. Compare the Observation Equivalence of these two systems. If both systems are observationally equivalent then it will display TRUE, otherwise some where in the LTS this property is not satisfied and terminate with FALSE result. Second method of verification is shown here in terms of SVL form.

(P1)   **observational comparison**
            strong reduction of
                total hide all but *read, write, du* **in**
                generation of "dsm.lotos"
        ==
        "prop1.aut"

Third method is property P1 written in mu-calculus and verified on DSM in LOTOS format. SVL provides this facility to verify property written in mu-calculus directly on LOTOS program.

In weak consistency, when ever Process P_i has been written some value then local memory has to update it. We will say this property as when ever Process P_i performed $write_i(a, d)$ operation then local memory updates $du_i(a, d)$ has to occur in the future states. We verified this property P2 in two ways. In first method, Property P2 written in mu-calculus form. Caesar

26

compiler convert LOTOS program of abstract DSM system into LTS System. We verified Property P2 on LTS. It will check in all possible cases in LTS. If this property satisfied in all cases then it will give TRUE result. If some where this property not satisfied then it will terminate with FASLE output. Property P2 written here in mu-calculus form.

(P2)   [true*. " write ". (not " du ")*. " du "] true

In second method of verifying property P2 is property written in mu-calculus and verified on DSM in LOTOS format. SVL provides this facility to verify property written in mucalculus directly on LOTOS program. For the remaining properties, we defined synchronization operation. In weak consistency, operations are divided into ordinary operations and synchronization operations. Formal specification of this property specified here in terms of $\forall$CTL.

(P2) $\forall(a,d) \in$ address $\times$ data, $\forall i \in$ index
$init \Rightarrow \mathbf{AG}[after(write(a,d)) \Rightarrow \mathbf{AF}(du(a,d))]$

In Weak Consistency, operations are divided into ordinary operations and synchronization operations. Property P3 consist of synchronization operation and previous two properties P1 and P2 consist of only ordinary operations. Third property of weak consistency is before an ordinary read or write access is allowed to perform with respect to any other processor; all previous synchronization accesses must be performed. Whenever we want to access ordinary read or write access all previous synchronization accesses must be complete then only we will to perform ordinary read or write operations. Synchronization accesses must be identified by the programmer or compiler in weak consistency. We need to ensure that data must be consistent at those synchronization accesses. This property is divided into two parts because this property involves two operations read or write operations and CADP doesn't provide a facility to verify property that involves two operations. So we divided this property into two parts and verified. Part A of property P3 is before an ordinary read access is allowed to perform with respect to any other processor; all previous synchronization accesses must be performed. Formal specification of property P3A is specified here in terms of $\forall$CTL.

(P3A) $\forall(a,d) \in$ address $\times$ data, $\forall i \in$ index
$init \Rightarrow \mathbf{AG}[before(read(a,d)) \Rightarrow \mathbf{A}(avail(prev(sync))]$

27

Part B of Property P3 is before an ordinary write access is allowed to perform with respect to any other processor; all previous synchronization accesses must be performed. Formal specification of property P3B is specified here in terms of ∀CTL.

(P3B) $\forall$(a,d) $\in$ address $\times$ data, $\forall$i $\in$ index
           $init \Rightarrow \mathbf{AG}[before(write(a,d)) \Rightarrow \mathbf{A}(avail(\ prev(\ sync\ ))]$

These properties include synchronization operations. So we defined user defined synchronization operation like read and write operations and then verified these properties using user defined synchronization operations. LO-TOS provides built in synchronization operations with help of that also we verified properties P3A and P3B. We verified properties P3A and P3B in four ways. In first method, we have written properties P3A and P3B in mu-calculus form. Caesar compiler converts abstract DSM in LOTOS form to LTS in BCG from. We verified properties P3A and P3B on LTS. Properties P3A and P3B checks in all the states in LTS then will give a result whether these properties are satisfied in all cases or not. If this property is satisfied in all the cases then terminated with TRUE result, otherwise terminate with FALSE. In second method, we have written properties P3A and P3B in alternation free mu-calculus form and then verified these properties directly on abstract DSM in LOTOS form. SVL provides this facility to verify properties with help of that we verified these properties. In verification of properties, first two methods we used user defined synchronization operation and remaining two methods i.e. third and fourth methods used built in synchronization operation. Properties P3A and P3B are written here in mu-calculus form.

(P3A)   [true* . " s " . (not " du ")* . "read"] false
(P3B)   [true* . " s " . (not " du ")* . "write"] false

In Weak Consistency, before synchronization access is allowed to perform with respect to any other processor; all previous ordinary READ and WRITE accesses must be performed. This property also divided into two parts. Part A is before synchronization access is allowed to perform with respect to any other processor; all previous ordinary READ accesses must be performed. Formal specification of property P4A is specified here in terms of ∀CTL

(P4A) $\forall$(a,d) $\in$ address $\times$ data, $\forall$i $\in$ index
           $init \Rightarrow \mathbf{AG}[before(sync) \Rightarrow avail(\ prev(\ read(a,d)))]$

28

Part B of this property is before synchronization access is allowed to perform with respect to any other processor; all previous ordinary WRITE accesses must be performed. Formal specification of property P4B is specified here in terms of ∀CTL

(P4B)   ∀(a,d) ∈ address × data, ∀i ∈ index
          $init \Rightarrow \mathbf{AG}[before(sync) \Rightarrow avail(\ prev(\ write(a,d)))]$

This property also includes synchronization operation. We verified this property also through user defined and built in synchronization operation. We verified this property in four ways. First method of verifying this property is we wrote property P4A and P4B in mu-calculus form, and then Caesar compiler converts abstract DSM in lotos form to LTS in BCG form. We verified properties P4A and P4B on LTS. It will give the results whether these properties are true or false. In second method of verifying these properties, we have written properties P4A and P4B in mu-calculus form, and then verified directly on abstract DSM in lotos form. SVL provides this facility to verify properties with help that we verified these properties P4A and P4B. These previous two methods of verifying properties we used user defined synchronization operations. The next two methods of verifying properties same as previous two methods here instead of user defined synchronization operation we used built in synchronization operation. we have written properties P4A and P4B in mu-calculus form here.

(P4A)   [true*. "read" . (not " du ")* . " s "] false
(P4B)   [true*. "write" . (not " du ")* . " s "] false

The last property is synchronization accesses are sequentially consistent with respect to one another. Our abstract DSM model, synchronization operation occurred then complete the all operations occurred up to that point then only we proceed further. For example, one synchronization operation occurred first then it has to wait until all previous operations complete, then second synchronization operation occurred. Obviously, these synchronization operations are sequentially consistent with respect to one another. In sequential consistency one operation occurred and its completed then only we will go for another operations. Here in synchronization operation case also same thing happened. So synchronization operations are sequentially consistent with respect to one another.

In the verification of DSM Weak Consistency properties, we have increased the number of processes and experimented. The experimental statistics of states, transitions and memory required in the generation of DSM with increased number of processes are shown in Table 4.1. we have applied

No.of Process	States	Transitions	Size(in KB)
3	25	110	3.1
4	41	212	4
5	76	403	4.8
10	236	1366	11.2
20	662	4281	21.3
30	1142	7549	31.4
40	2086	13867	40.8

Table 4.1: Increased number of processes before Strong Reduction

strong reduction on the generation of DSM and its results are shown in Table 4.2. So memory is not a constraint even we increase number of processes.

No.of Process	States	Transitions	Size(in KB)
3	12	24	2.5
4	22	53	2.7
5	44	228	3.1
10	159	828	8.4
20	493	3314	14.8
30	865	6094	22.1
40	1704	11981	29.7

Table 4.2: Increased number of processes after Strong Reduction

4.3   Verification Model

We implemented Abstract DSM System in LOTOS (dsm.lotos) which includes all operations that is sufficient to verify weak consistency properties. Caesar compiler will convert from lotos program to labeled transition system (LTS) in binary coded graph format (BCG). If we run a program under Aldebaran option (Caesar aldebaran) then it will convert lotos program to LTS in aldebaran (aut) format. Weak Consistency properties are written in temporal languages like XTL, mu-calculus and these properties are verified in LTS of abstract DSM System; get a TRUE/FALSE answer for each property. If abstract DSM satisfies the property then we will get a true otherwise false. We wrote a script file for this whole process in SVL format. Once we run the script file whole process was done and TRUE/FALSE result will displayed. The model is illustrated in Figure 4.2.

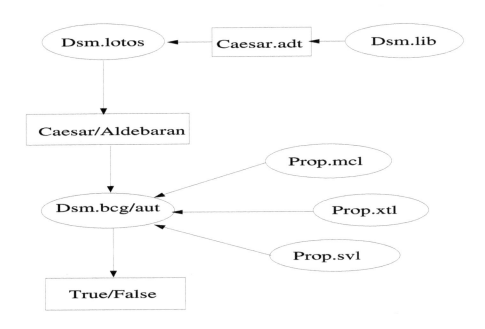

Figure 4.2: Verification Model of Weak Consistency properties

4.4   Output Snapshots

Output Shanpshots are shown in Figures 4.3 and 4.4.

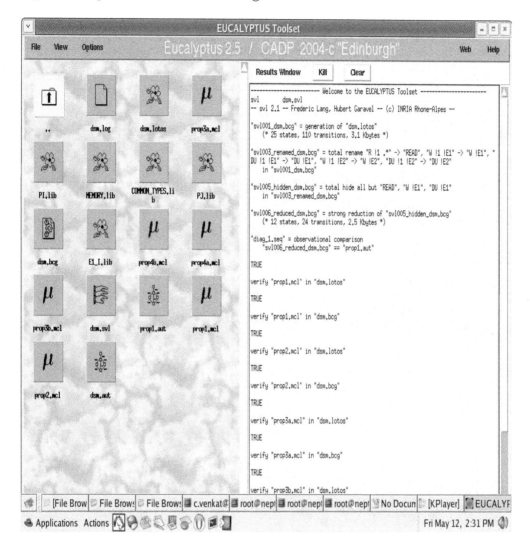

Figure 4.3: Output Snapshot1

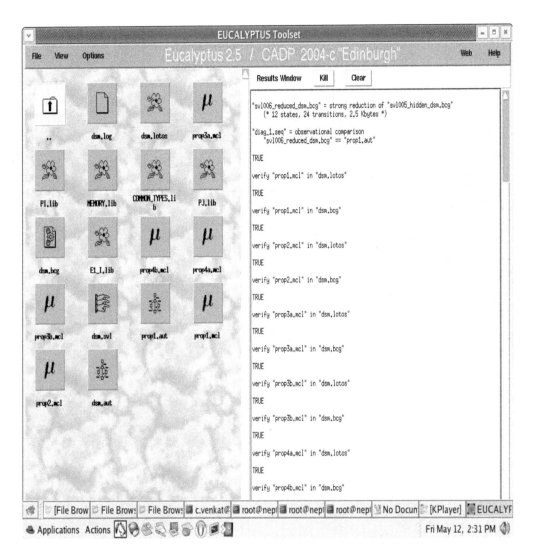

Figure 4.4: Output Snapshot2

Chapter 5

Conclusion

Conclusion: In DSM System, data consistency is one of the key issue. We have to maintain data as consistent when multiple processes are accessing the shared memory. We have to explore the all possible errors and thorough testing of data consistency in DSM system is essential. The best possible way to do that is formal verification of DSM consistency models. Sequential Consistency unnecessarily reduces the performance of the system because it does not allow to reorder or pipelining the memory operations. Relaxed Consistency allows reordering of memory events and buffering or pipelining of memory accesses. So that Relaxed Consistency improves the performance of the DSM system. As part of verification of Relaxed Consistency models, we

- Desinged and Implemented Abstract Distributed Shared memory Sytem

- Specified and Verified properties of DSM Weak Consistency model using CADP Toolbox.

So that it increase our confidence in the correctness of DSM Relaxed Consistency models.

Bibliography

[1] E.M.Clarke, O. Grumberg, and D.A. Peled, *Model Checking*, The MIT Press, 2nd Edition, 2000.

[2] S.Rajan, N.Shankar, and M.K.Srivas, An Integration of model checking with automated proof checking, *Proc. of the 7th International Conference on Computer Aided Verification*, LNCS, Vol. 939, pp. 84-97, 1995.

[3] M.J. Elynn, *Computer Architecture: Pipelined and Parallel Processor Design*, ISBN 0-86720-204-1, Jones and Bartlett Publishers, 1995.

[4] V. Lo, Operating Systems Enhancements for Distributed Shared Memory, *Advances in Computers*, Vol. 39, pp. 191-237, 1994.

[5] Protic, Tomasevic, and Milutinovic, Distributed Shared Memory: Concepts and Systems, *IEEE Parallel and Distributed Technology*, Vol. 4, pp. 63-79, 1996.

[6] P. Chatterjee, H. Sivaraj, and G. Gopalakrishnan, Shared Memory Consistency Protocol Verification Against Weak Memory Models: Refinement via Model Checking, *Proc. of the 14th International Conference on Computer Aided Verification*, LNCS, Vol. 2404, pp. 123-136, 2002.

[7] Sarita V. Adve and K. Gharachorloo, Shared Memory Consistency Models: A Tutorial, *IEEE Computer Society Press*, Vol. 29, pp. 66-76, 1996.

[8] Leslie Lamport, How to make a multiprocessor computer that correctly executes multiprocessor programs, *Proc. of the 1992 ACM/IEEE conference on Supercomputing*, IEEE Transactions on Computers, Vol. 28, pp. 241-248, 1979.

[9] James R. Goodman, Cache consistency and sequential consistency, Technical Report no. 61, SCI Committee, March 1989.

[10] M. Dubois, C. Scheurich, and F. Briggs, Memory access buffering in multiprocessors, *Proc. of the 13th Annual International Symposium on Computer Architecture*, pp. 434-442, 1986.

[11] K. Gharachorloo, D. E. Lenoski, J. Laudon, P. Gibbons, A. Gupta, and J. L. Hennessy, Memory consistency and event ordering in scalable shared-memory multiprocessors, *Proc. of the 17th Annual International Symposium on Computer Architecture*, pp. 15-26, 1990.

[12] P. Keleher, A.L. Cox, and W. Zwaenepoel, Lazy release consistency for software distributed shared memory, *Proc. of the 19th Annual International Symposium on Computer Architecture*, pp. 13-21, 1992.

[13] B.N. Bershad, M. J. Zekauskas, and W. A. Sawdon, The Midway Distributed Shared Memory System, *Proc. of IEEE COMPCON Conference*, pp. 528-537, 1993.

[14] Yong-Kim Chong and Kai Hwang, Performance Analysis of Four Memory Consistency Models for Multithreaded Multiprocessors, *IEEE Transaction on Parallel and Distributed Systems*, Vol. 6, pp. 1085-1099, 1995.

[15] J. Protic and V. Milutinovic. Entry Consistency versus Lazy Release Consistency in DSM Systems: Analytical Comparison and a New Hybrid Solution, *6th IEEE Workshop on Future Trends of Distributed Computing Systems*, pp. 78-83, 1997.

[16] Susanne Graf, Characterization of a Sequentially Consistent Memory and Verification of a Cache Memory by Abstraction, *Distributed Computing Journal*, Vol. 12, pp. 75-90, 1999.

[17] Rob Gerth, Sequential consistency and the lazy caching algorithm, *Distributed computing journal*, Vol. 12, pp. 57-59, 1999.

[18] T. Henzinger, S. Qadeer, and S. Rajamani. Verifying sequential consistency on shared-memory multiprocessor systems, *Proc. of the 11th International Conference on Computer Aided Verification*, LNCS, Vol. 1633, pp. 301-315, 1999.

[19] S. Qadeer, Verifying sequential consistency on shared-memory multiprocessors by Model Checking, *IEEE Transactions on Parallel and Distributed Systems*, Vol. 14, pp. 730-741, 2003.

[20] A. Condon and Alan J. Hu, Automatable verification of sequential consistency, *ACM Symposium on Parallel Algorithms and Architectures*, pp. 113-121, 2001.

[21] P. Chatterjee and G. Gopalakrishnan, A Specification and Verification Framework for Developing Weak Shared Memory Consistency Protocols, *Proc. of the 4th International Conference on Formal Methods in Computer-Aided Design*, LNCS, Vol. 2517, pp. 292-309, 2002.

[22] R.P. Ghughal1 and G. Gopalakrishnan, Verification Methods for Weaker Shared Memory Consistency Models, *Proc. of the 15 IPDPS 2000 Workshops on Parallel and Distributed Processing*, LNCS, Vol. 1800, pp. 985-992, 2000.

[23] http://www.inrialpes.fr/vasy/cadp/

[24] Tommaso Bolognesi and Ed Brinksma, Introduction to the ISO Specification Language LOTOS, *Computer Networks and ISDN Systems*, vol. 14, pp. 25-59, 1987.

[25] M. A. Ardis, Lessons from using basic LOTOS, *Proc. of the 16th international conference on Software engineering*, IEEE Computer Society Press, pp. 5-14, 1994.

[26] H. Garavel and J. Sifakis, Compilation and Verification of LOTOS Specifications, *Proc. of the 10th International Symposium on Protocol Specification, Testing and Verification*, pp. 379-394, 1990.

[27] Hubert Garavel, Compilation of LOTOS Abstract Data Types, *Proc. of the 2nd International Conference on Formal Description Techniques*, pp. 147-162, 1989.

[28] J.Claude Fernandez, Aldebaran: A Tool for Verification of Communicating Processes, Rapport SPECTRE, C14, Laboratoire de Gnie Informatique - Institut IMAG, Grenoble, September 1989.

[29] Louis-Pascal Tock, The BCG PostScript Format, Rapport SPECTRE, INRIA Rhne-Alpes, Grenoble, October 1995.

[30] R. Mateescu and H. Garavel, XTL: A Meta-Language and Tool for Temporal Logic Model-Checking, *Proc. of the International Workshop on Software Tools for Technology Transfer*, 1998.

[31] http://www.inrialpes.fr/vasy/eucalyptus.html

[32] H. Garavel and F. Lang, SVL: a Scripting Language for Compositional Verification, *Proc. of the 21st IFIP WG 6.1 International Conference on Formal Techniques for Networked and Distributed Systems*, 2001.

[33] http://www.inrialpes.fr/vasy/cadp/man/evaluator.html

[34] http://www.inrialpes.fr/vasy/cadp/man/tgv.html

www.ingramcontent.com/pod-product-compliance
Lightning Source LLC
LaVergne TN
LVHW081532050326
832903LV00025B/1762